Mighty Machines
Submarines

by Jennifer Reed

Consulting Editor: Gail Saunders-Smith, PhD

Capstone
press

Mankato, Minnesota

Pebble Plus is published by Capstone Press,
151 Good Counsel Drive, P.O. Box 669, Mankato, Minnesota 56002.
www.capstonepress.com

1 2 3 4 5 6 12 11 10 09 08 07

Library of Congress Cataloging-in-Publication Data
Reed, Jennifer, 1967–
    Submarines/ by Jennifer Reed.
    p.cm—(Pebble Plus. Mighty machines)
    "Summary: Simple text and photographs describe submarines, their parts, and what they do"—Provided
by publisher.
    Includes bibliographical references and index.
    ISBN-13: 978-1-4296-0031-6 (hardcover)
    ISBN-10: 1-4296-0031-4 (hardcover)
1. Submarines—Juvenile literature. I. Title. II. Series.
V857 .R44 2008
623.82—dc22   2006101336

Capstone Press thanks Dr. Sarandis Papadopoulos, Naval Historian, for his assistance with this book.

Editorial Credits
Mari Schuh and Erika L. Shores, editors; Patrick D. Dentinger, book designer; Jo Miller, photo researcher

Photo Credits
Check Six/Erik Simonsen, 21
DVIC, cover; Chris Oxley (NNSD), 8–9; Don S. Montgomery, 13 (inset); JOC Peter D. Sundberg, 19;
    JOSN Brandon Shelander, 14–15; Paul Farley, 10–11; PH2 Scott Taylor, 7
Photo provided courtesy General Dynamics Electric Boat, 1
U.S. D.O.D. graphic by Ron Stern, 4–5
U.S. Navy photo, 16–17
U.S. Navy photo by Mr. Paul Farley, 13

Note to Parents and Teachers

The Mighty Machines set supports national social studies standards related to science, technology, and society. This book describes and illustrates submarines. The images support early readers in understanding the text. The repetition of words and phrases helps early readers learn new words. This book also introduces early readers to subject-specific vocabulary words, which are defined in the Glossary section. Early readers may need assistance to read some words and to use the Table of Contents, Glossary, Read More, Internet Sites, and Index sections of the book.

Table of Contents

What Are Submarines?

Submarines are ships
that move underwater.
They are also called subs.

Subs have a long body

called a hull.

A fin on top

is called a sail.

hull

sail

Parts of Subs

Subs have propellers

to move fast in the water.

Subs have tanks
that fill with air.
The air helps subs
float in the water.

Subs have periscopes
inside their sails.
Periscopes help crews
see other ships.

periscopes

What Subs Do

Submarines have machines
to tell if other ships
are close.
The machines can also tell
how deep the water is.

Some subs shoot missiles
during battles.
Underwater missiles
are called torpedoes.

Small subs help people
learn about the ocean.
Crew members study
objects deep underwater.

Mighty Machines

Subs dive deep
into the water.
Subs are
mighty machines.

Glossary

float—to rest on water

hull—the main body of a ship or boat

missile—a weapon that blows up when it hits a target

periscope—a long tube with mirrors at each end; submarine crews use periscopes to view their surroundings in all directions.

propeller—a set of spinning blades that pushes ships through water

sail—the finlike part on top of a submarine

Read More

Lock, Deborah. *Submarines and Submersibles*. DK Readers. Beginning to Read. New York: DK, 2007.

Stone, Lynn M. *Submarines at Sea: Fighting Forces*. Fighting Forces on the Sea. Vero Beach, Fla.: Rourke, 2006.

Internet Sites

FactHound offers a safe, fun way to find Internet sites related to this book. All of the sites on FactHound have been researched by our staff.

Here's how:

1. Visit *www.facthound.com*

2. Choose your grade level.

3. Type in this book ID **1429600314** for age-appropriate sites. You may also browse subjects by clicking on letters, or by clicking on pictures and words.

4. Click on the **Fetch It** button.

FactHound will fetch the best sites for you!

Index

Word Count: 118
Grade: 1
Early-Intervention Level: 12